MEDITATION

The Ten Step

Path

Linda T Levine

Preface

With the current state of the world, the numerous fears, and the uncertainty, what can we do to escape and find a source of instant relaxation? There is somewhere, a well-kept secret and only a few have access. What would you give to find such a place?

By following the instructions in this book and listening to the guided meditations, you will soon learn how beneficial it is to feed the mind, as well as the body. In just minutes and with three special breaths, you will be transported into tranquillity.

With this easily learned system you will begin to feel calm, composed, and confident. You will find that by breathing mindfully in a special sequence, you will become stress-free, more creative and experience improved productivity

Contents

Meditation is a source of inner peace,

inner peace is a source of happiness.

Dance with Meditation

My dance with meditation began on the day that I injured my back and was unable to take a single step for several months. It was an ordinary summer's day in 1987. I remember it well. There were no parking spaces outside the store, and I was getting stressed. I double-parked, opened the door and the puppy, who had been perched on the back seat, jumped out into the road. My heart missed a beat and I leapt out after her and grabbed her by the scruff of the neck as a car sped past. At that moment, an excruciating sensation shot across my lower back and I felt something go 'ping'. Clutching the puppy in my arms, I scrambled back into the driver's seat and drove slowly home. That night I drifted in and out of troubled sleep.

The next morning as I attempted to get out of bed, I collapsed on the floor with the most unbearable pain, it felt as if a hot poker had been inserted into my, spine and the pain was shooting down my right leg. During the months that followed the pain became progressively worse and the stress was uncontrollable. Following an MRI scan, the surgeon informed me that due to the severity of the ruptured disc and damaged sciatic nerve there would be on alternative but to operate; he added my name to the waiting list. I knew that it would be a long time before I would be able to dance again.

After a few weeks a friend came to visit, and I frantically repeated the prognosis that had been given to me. My friend looked at me solemnly and announced, "You need to relax!" To be honest, I was about to tell him to leave. How could I relax when I was in constant pain? "Have you ever tried to meditate?" he said, almost apologetically. I looked at him in disbelief, I was unable to walk and he was talking about meditation. The next evening my friend returned and presented me with a cassette recording. "Listen to this!" he said. He sat on the floor crossed legged and switched on the cassette player. I remained in my usual position, flat on my back. The sound of soft music drifted around the room and the tender; soothing words of a man's voice weaved their way into my mind. It was the first time listening to a guided meditation. I closed my eyes and allowed my mind to follow him as he led me away from the stress and pain. The tension melted, my muscles relaxed, my mind became clear and all that I could hear was the sound of my own dancing heartbeat. It was a slow process, but as the weeks turned into months, the pain lessened, and I slowly regained mobility. Throughout the experience, my meditation practice increased.

Two years later, I was invited to attend an event at the NEC in Birmingham, hosted by motivational trainer Anthony Robbins. In the weeks before the event, we were encouraged to meditate daily. It was an interesting seminar, concluding on the last evening with an organised fire-walk. Firewalking has been practised by people from different cultures for thousands of years, it is understood to have been happening in India around 1200 BC. Whilst it certainly compares to mind over matter, the act of walking across hot coals is a symbolic experience and aims to give people the courage to take on any challenges that life presents. With the rationale, if they can walk across fire, they can make it through anything. It was an event that I would never forget. The long bed of hot embers crackled and sizzled. Everyone, including the seminar participants and staff teams, had completed the walk. It was a damp, November night and I stood alone, contemplating, and considering what might happen to my feet. A deep, husky voice spoke gently and reassuringly. "You can do it," said

Anthony Robbins, smiling down at me. "Just keep repeating over and over in your mind, cool moss!'' It is a way of directing the mind with the expectation that you will feel the coolness of the moss underfoot, instead of focusing the mind on the embers. I closed my eyes and took a deep breath and started to chant "cool moss''. I stepped forward and glided, floated, and danced across the hot coals. When I eventually reached the end of the ember bed, someone directed me to a large container of cold water, to cool my feet. That experience certainly created a sense of empowerment.

Meditation has remained my constant friend always finding a way to dance into my life, especially, at times of stress. It was at the end of March 2020 that my 'dance' changed from a waltz routine to one with the intensity of a tango. Alone, in the solitary confinement called self-shielding, the overwhelming sadness was difficult to endure. During the months that followed, meditation became my lifeline helping to create mindfulness in every moment, being present with the feelings and thoughts and having the awareness to breathe them away. It is my wish that you too will discover the benefits that meditation has to offer.

What is Meditation?

Meditation can be described as a mental process of stilling the mind, a time to switch off from distracting thoughts. Once mastered, will provide lasting benefits. In today's fast-paced, stress-filled life, we all need to find the joy of inner peace and to be able to access it anytime and anyplace. Just as one would visit the gym to help strengthen the body or the spa to relax the muscles, meditation helps to focus, strengthen and relax the mind.

There are various meditations techniques, *i.e.,* Guided Visualisation, Transcendental Meditation and Mindfulness, and different ways to meditate, *i.e.,* breath-work, focus single-pointedly on an object and mantra. (*descriptions are to be found in the Glossary at the end of this book*). The Ten Step Meditation course uses a simple, enjoyable, effective technique that will create positive benefits almost immediately.

The wonderful thing about meditation is that once mastered it can be practised anytime and anywhere. The art of mindfulness is to reach a stage whereby we can introduce it into our everyday life and not only when we are enjoying the meditation practice. With learning to become aware of the breath and to quiet the mind from all the many demanding distractions, we will enjoy better general health, improve the quality of our sleep, be more creative and cope more productively with daily challenges in a calm and relaxed way.

Meditation in some form or another is now practised by thousands of people from all walks of life across the globe. Whilst there are many forms of meditation, the main purpose is to train the mind in clarity and stillness. In this way, we learn how to let go of worrying thoughts and excessive stress. When our mind is filled with this type of thinking we are prone to develop feelings of anger, frustration, fear and other negative characteristics that cause us to remain is an unproductive state. If this is left unchecked and continues it can lead to serious consequences that may affect a person's mental health and in turn impact close relationships in a damaging way.

Therefore, training the mind to settle, rather than constantly following negative thoughts help to give rise to feelings of happiness, calmness and peace. This allows us to take the time to step back and evaluate a situation without reacting in a non-productive way. Through the process of learning to let go of unwanted thoughts, we find that we have more energy to do the things that we enjoy and enjoy the things that we do.

The Ten Step Meditation course has many benefits. However, we do need to develop a routine. Through using this method that is simple to learn, enjoyable to do and fits in neatly with a busy daily schedule, once we have become skilful with the basic idea and have experienced blissful relaxation, we may wish to develop the experience deeper. Therefore, it is recommended to extend the practice to longer periods of time; gradually increasing from five to twenty minutes for each of the ten meditations. It is also possible to practice for five minutes per session, using the Three-Step Breath exercise several times a day.

Sunrise over the lake

The Three-Step Breath

The *Three-Step Breath* is a special way of learning to control the breath and a powerful way of calming the mind. Once the initial three-step breathing exercise has been learnt and we have become familiar with stilling the mind any activity can be carried out mindfully, directing our attention to the present moment and keeping us in full awareness. This simple act of paying attention will help to stop the mind from wandering and keep us focused and more relaxed.

Therapeutic benefits of meditation will soon become clear. By quieting the mind, we let go of confusion, the memory improves and increases clearer thinking with more creativity and a happier mental attitude. Meditation can contribute to achieving these much-longed-for results.

We can begin to introduce mindfulness into our regular activities throughout the day, *i.e.*, mindful walking, showering, eating, brushing the hair, cooking, listening to relaxing music, in fact, the list can go on. However, the important aspect of meditation is not the type that we practice, moreover it is the willingness and intention that create the best results. A skill can be learnt as with everything and meditation is no different.

Once learnt, Three-Step Breath training will be especially beneficial if practised before going to sleep at night. It will help to create a routine for the body and mind, gradually increasing the duration from five minutes to a maximum of twenty minutes. It can also be helpful to keep a special place where you will regularly practice meditation.

Ensure that it is a quiet place where you will feel comfortable and be able to relax without being disturbed. Always be mindful of your surroundings trying not to feel too hot nor too cold. Some people find it comforting to wrap a shawl around their shoulders or across their knees. There are no fixed ways to be seated, whatever you feel the most comfortable. either on a chair or crossed-legged on the floor. However, the back must be straight and upright. Keep the intention to remain focused and the willingness to become stress-free and happy. Be kind and patient with yourself.

During meditation, the mind will wander, the skill is not to follow the thoughts, but instead to simply observe and let them go. A good way to do this is to imagine that thoughts are like clouds that appear in the clear sky with the understanding that they will soon disappear, and you can learn to watch them float away. Over time and with determination this will become easier. If practised as recommended, and regularly, it will help both physically and emotionally. It is something that everyone, including children, can learn to do and it can be practised alone, with family and friends, listening to the recordings, or in an organised meditation group.

The benefits include restful sleep, increased creativity, better relationships, less anger, a happier and more peaceful mind. The positive results that we gain from learning to meditate may encourage others to become interested and the more that we incorporate mindfulness into our daily lives the happier our environment will become.

Waiting for the clouds to float away

Three Step Breath
Overview

The Three Step Breathing exercise is a special method of working with the breath mindfully, consisting of the inhalation, suspending the breath and then exhalation. Once this process has been learnt correctly, it is the basis for most meditations and the results of this practice are ten-fold. The full instructions are to be found further along in the book, and throughout the meditation coursework.

About Meditation

Much has been written supporting the efficacy of meditation and mindfulness as a regular practice. Trials have been run and monitoring has been carried out in laboratory settings to support the function of the brain patterns and the positive changes that occur amongst regular meditators. Therefore, I would greatly encourage you to experience meditation for yourself and you will find how beneficial it is.

Of course, I am biased because I have been practising meditation for many years, more than three decades to be exact. It is wonderful to witness the current interest from the medical, academic and scientific communities involving the beneficial practice of training the mind to achieve positive and life-enhancing results.

Personal experience is always the best route to follow. To gain the most benefits, this will only be achieved through commitment and regular practice, however, some people do experience immediate and positive results.

The course has been developed for the beginner and will start with the basic understanding that is fundamental for most schools of meditation and mindfulness. Throughout the Ten Step Meditation course, participants will be guided through a program that will strengthen their understanding of how to meditate in a simple yet deep way. Each step follows a natural progression from the previous one. The program can be customised to the individual without losing any of the benefits.

It is possible to practice each step simultaneously during a ten-day period. However, it would be suitable and is recommended to work with each of the ten steps at a pace of one week per meditation, thus creating the complete ten-week course. In this way the participant would have developed the necessary skills to advance to the final tenth step meditation. It is strongly advised that the participant practices each step several times before proceeding to the next one, and before participating in the final Step Ten of this course.

The History of Meditation

Meditation, according to archaeologic reports dates back as early as 5,000 BCE. Whilst the practice of meditation is rooted in many different religions globally, including the ancient Egyptians, Judaism, Hinduism and Buddhism. Mindful methods can be traced back two thousand six hundred years to life and times of Buddha Shakyamuni. He was a scholar and spiritual master. It is from his direct teachings that have been handed down from disciple to disciple and by the many great masters across the ages, that mindfulness of today has developed.

Jon Kabat Zinn, a professor of medicine, pioneered the MBSR course and was the first to put it into practice at the University of Massachusetts Medical School. He was a student of Zen Buddhism and studied with Buddhist master Tich Nhat Hahn. It was through his understanding and teachings that led him to integrate the studies with scientific evidence and create the Mindfulness Based Stress Reduction program that is recognised globally today. He introduced the benefits of a mindfulness practice without any religious overtones to the wider public and scientific communities on a global scale. MBSR is now offered alongside talking therapies by many medical centres, hospitals and various organisations. Most recently, an adaptation of the course has been developed for schools, addressing the needs of both younger children and teenagers. There are now teacher training courses available at the university level.

During the latter part of the 20th century it developed into a more stylish than spiritual practice, to the point where technology has now become involved and Apps are available to download. People from all walks of life are using mindfulness as a tool for training the mind and helping overcome many of the modern-day causes of stress, depression and insomnia.

November Sky 2020

Inspirational quotes

"Life is a dance. Mindfulness is witnessing that dance"

Amit Ray

"Our life is shaped by our mind, for we become what we think"

Buddha

"Do not dwell in the past, do not dream of the future, concentrate the mind on the present moment"

Buddha

Introduction to the course

We are all able to access inner peace simply because we all breathe

The Ten Step Meditation program has been designed as a complete course, starting with an introduction to the basic technique of meditation. It is based on a simplified version and combination of mindfulness and guided visualisations. It is structured so that we become familiar with the Three Step Breath, this in-itself will be beneficial helping to bring a change that can alleviate stressful thoughts, so often the cause for disrupted sleep patterns. We will learn how to recognise and defuse the 'time bomb' before it explodes into a state of stress, anger, or panic. Instead, we will be encouraged to learn how to train the mind to relax. During the process we will become more mindful with happier relationships, better quality sleep, enhanced imagination, have overall better health and improve and sharpen memory.

All the meditations are available as recordings for download and can be accessed through the website or by contacting us directly. Details are available at the end of the book. To gain full benefits of this course it is recommended that you practice regularly. For the duration of the course it is beneficial to keep a journal, in this way we observe what works and how to develop the practice further. As we become familiar with various meditation and relaxation techniques we are learning to understand and train the mind.

Clouds

During meditation, the mind will wander, the skill is not to follow the thoughts, but instead, to simply observe as they go. A good way to do this is to imagine that thoughts are like clouds that appear in the clear sky, with the understanding that they will soon disappear you can watch as they slowly float away. Over time and with practise this exercise will become easier and it is extremely beneficial.

If you look carefully into this picture you may see a face

or two

The First Breath of Life

What is sound that beats across time?
Echoes softly, yet before the first breath of life is taken,
When deep and safe within a sacred place of creation
Even in the darkness, somehow, a tiny speck of life so new
Will get to know the vibration beating to and fro
The first sound ever heard, the chanting of a drum
Long before the first breath of life?

A tiny seed begins to form, a miracle in every way
Protected in your water world; this is the only world you
have known,
Has been this way since the dawn of time, never will it
change
As you remain concealed, deep within your ocean,
The only sound you may hear, the beating of a distant drum
Long before the first breath of life.

And when in time all knowledge and wisdom has been
stored within,

Beholding all the wonders of creation,

The time is right for you to leave the safety of the sacred place;

Innocent of the world you will have to face

Your home of water has gone

Will you recall the sound of the drum:

Your mother's heartbeat Before you took the first breath of life?

Linda Levine 2015

Ten Step Meditation Path

During the first meditation step, we will discover the breath of life. It can be used throughout the meditation practice and whenever it is needed at any time during the day or night. It is extremely beneficial to practice for several minutes before going to sleep and first thing in the morning. It is a wonderful tool for calming the mind and relaxing the body. The fact that we all breathe means that we are all able to meditate. If we can meditate, we can relax and if we can relax, we can be calm and happy. However, the breath is something that we take for granted.

You will find it most beneficial if you can perform this first step in mindful breathing at least three times a day. As you become more familiar with the process, you will find that it is possible to practice anywhere and at any time, but for now let us begin by being in an undisturbed, quiet place.

The Meditations
Step One: Breath of Life

Now that you are set to begin, find a quiet place where you will not be disturbed, switch off your phone and focus your intention on wanting to relax. Ensure that the room is comfortably warm and give yourself this precious time to unwind. Sit in a comfortable position, either on the floor or on a chair with your back straight. If you are sitting on a chair, try to ensure that your feet are flat on the ground. Your hands resting in your lap or on your knees. When you feel ready close your eyes.

Bring your attention to the breath and become aware as it enters in and then out through the nostrils. Do not try to control the breath, only have the realisation that you are breathing.

Feel the breath as it flows in and out of your body. Notice any difference when it enters the nostrils and when it leaves. Does it feel cooler on the in-breath, warmer on the exhalation?

Continue breathing in and out with mindful curiosity. If you find that your mind is wandering try not to follow the thought, instead just notice as it goes, returning your attention to the sensation of the breath entering and leaving the body. Every time a thought comes up, continue to just observe it and let it go. Gently directing your focus back to the sensation of the breath, following the flow as it goes in and out of the nostrils. Continue in this way for several minutes. Slowly inhale, and on the out-breath let go of any tension and feel your shoulders relaxing. Breathing gently and naturally keeping your focus on the steady flow of breath.

Take a breath in and on the out-breath feel your tummy relaxing. Remain aware and try to stay focused as you breathe in, and as you breathe out feel your face relaxing.

Breathe in, allow the breath to become a little deeper and then slowly exhale. Again, breathe in a little deeper and slowly exhale. Once more, breathe in gently and deeply with awareness. Exhale through the nostrils.

Continue to breathe naturally and when you feel ready, without the need to rush, slowly open your eyes. Be curious and notice how you are feeling. Are there any changes in your body and mind from when first you started the meditation? Be kind and patient with yourself and try to perform this exercise again during the day or last thing at night.

Meditation

Step Two: Mindful Breathing

Now that you are set to begin, find a quiet place where you will not be disturbed, switch off your phone and focus your intention on wanting to relax. Ensure that the room is comfortably warm and give yourself this precious time to unwind. Sit in a comfortable position, either on the floor or on a chair with your back straight. If you are sitting on a chair, try to ensure that your feet are flat on the ground. Your hands resting in your lap or on your knees. When you feel ready close your eyes and become aware of the breath as it enters in and then out through the nostrils.

Do not try to control the breath, only have the realisation that you are breathing.

Close your eyes, feel the breath as it flows gently in and out of your body.

As you take the next breath in through your nostrils allow it to become slower and deeper, as you breathe out, feel the muscles around your jaw and in your face **relaxing**. Breathe in slowly and deeply, as you slowly breathe out, feel your shoulders relaxing and letting go of any tension.

Focus your attention on to the breath and with your awareness follow it as it enters your body. Bring it all the way down to your tummy and as you breathe out release any tension from that area of your body and feel the muscles relaxing. Try to remain with the breath and notice where in your body do you feel the flow, is it in your chest, your tummy? Continue to take long, slow mindful breaths. On your next deep breath in following it all the way down to your feet and the tips of the toes, you can use your awareness or imagination. Notice any sensations that you feel in this area. You may feel warmth, tingling, some movement or perhaps no sensations at all. Whatever you feel is fine and a personal experience, all that you need do is notice what you are feeling and if your mind wanders bring it back to the present moment simply by taking a deep, slow breath in and returning to any sensations in your feet. As you slowly exhale, silently repeat, I am letting go of any tension that is in my feet and toes.

Take a long, slow, deep breath in and allow it to fill your legs and hips. Notice if there are any sensations. On the exhalation let go of any tension in this area of your body. Breathe in slowly and deeply, filing the legs and hips with the breath, as you slowly exhale repeat silently, I am letting go of any tension from my legs and hips. Feel that part of your body relaxing.

Taking a slow, deep breath in and fill the entire area of the torso. Be aware of the breath as it fills your tummy and chest. Notice any sensations in these areas. Heaviness, tightness or perhaps a feeling of warmth. If there are no specific sensations, that is fine, continue to notice the breath. As you slowly exhale imagine all the tension from your tummy and chest leaving your body with the out-breath. Take another slow, deep breath in and feel the tummy expand as it fills with the breath. You may wish to place a hand across your tummy and feel how it rises as you breathe in and how it falls when you exhale. Silently repeat, I am letting go of tension and stressful feelings.

Take another long, slow, deep inhalation and imagine it filling your arms, hands and fingers. Notice, are there any sensations, heaviness, tightness or perhaps no sensations at all? Be mindful and get a sense of how you are holding your hands, are they palms up, or clenched into a fist? With the exhalation slowly release and allow them to relax. Take a long, slow, deep breath in and as you slowly exhale repeat silently, I am letting go of tension and stress.
The back is a typical area for holding stress and tension and often will result in painful conditions. On the next long,

slow, deep inhalation imagine the breath is filling your back and shoulders and allow it to fill the whole area of that part of the body. Do your shoulders feel relaxed or are they tense, tight and hunched up? With the long, slow exhalation be certain to release any tightness or tension. Take a long, slow deep breath and fill the area of your back and shoulders once more. As you slowly and fully exhale repeat silently, I am letting go of stress, I am letting go of tension, I am letting go of any tightness.

The face is an area where we hold a lot of tension that displays itself in the form of lines, fine wrinkles and a sallow complexion. To look fresh and relaxed, it is important to promote a feeling of relaxation in the muscles of the face, neck and head. Be aware of any sensations in this part of the body. Take a long, slow, deep breath in and allow it to fill your face, neck and head. As you slowly and gently exhale imagine any tension and stressful thoughts being released with the out-breath. Take another deep, slow breath in, filling the face, neck and head. Exhale and release any stressful thoughts or tension that may still be lingering in your face, neck or head. Take a long, slow deep breath in and then slowly exhale repeating silently, I am letting go of stress, I am letting go of tension, I am letting go of any tightness, I am letting go of worries.

Take a long deep breath in and follow it all the way throughout your body, if the mind wanders gently bring your attention back to the breath and hold for a moment before you begin to slowly exhale. Your whole body is feeling lighter and more relaxed. Be mindful of how it feels.

When you feel ready, without rushing, in your own time open your eyes.

Try to keep this calm feeling as you continue with your daily tasks.

If you notice any tension arising during the day, be mindful and inhale slowly, as you exhale imagine the tension leaving your body with the out-breath. You can repeat this process as many times as you need during the day or night.

A clear blue sky above the Regent's Canal

Meditation
Step Three: Clear Blue Sky

Find a quiet place where you will not be disturbed, switch off your phone and focus your intention on wanting to relax. Ensure that the room is comfortably warm and give yourself this precious time to unwind. Sit in a comfortable position, either on the floor or on a chair with your back straight. If you are sitting on a chair, try to ensure that your feet are flat on the ground.

Begin by becoming aware of the breath as it enters in and then out through the nostrils. Do not try to control the breath, only have the realisation that you are breathing.

Close your eyes, feel the breath as it flows gently in and out of your body.

As you take the next breath in through your nostrils allow it to become slower and deeper, as you breathe out, feel the muscles around your jaw and in your face relaxing. Breathe in slowly and deeply, as you slowly breathe out, feel your shoulders relaxing and letting go of any tension.

Take a long, slow breath all the way down to your tummy, as you exhale let go of all the tension in your body. Allow it to leave your body with the out-breath. Continue to take long, slow, deep breaths, each time bringing the in-breath to fill the tummy and then slowly with the exhalation becoming more relaxed. Any thoughts that come into your mind try not to follow them; remaining as a mindful observer notice the thoughts and let them go. Each time bringing your attention back to the breath and continuing where you left off.

Visualise or imagine that your mind is like a clear blue sky, each thought that enters your mind is like a cloud that drifts past and then disappears. Some clouds will appear small and pass quickly, others may seem like dark, heavy rain clouds, but remember that they will soon pass and once again you will see a clear blue sky. Continue to focus your attention on each breath allowing the in-breath to become slower and deeper, hold the breath briefly, and then slowly exhale keeping the picture in your minds-eye of a clear blue sky. Take another slow, deep breath in and hold the breath briefly before you slowly exhale. We will continue to focus breathing on this sequence for a further 5 - 10 minutes. Gradually, the wandering mind and thoughts will lessen, and the clear sky will fill your mind with a feeling of calmness and relaxation.

Breathe in slowly and deeply, hold the breath for a moment and then slowly exhale. Each new inhalation becoming slower and deeper. Breathe in slowly and deeply, hold the breath for a few moments before slowly exhaling. Continue with the three-point breath for a maximum of ten minutes. Relax your concentration, take a slow, deep breath in and exhale.

Without the need to rush, slowly open your eyes. Have a stretch and when you feel ready continue with your day feeling relaxed and calm.

Meditation

Step Four: The Ocean Breath

Find a quiet place where you will not be disturbed, switch off your phone and focus your intention on wanting to relax. Ensure that the room is comfortably warm and give yourself this precious time to unwind. Sit in a comfortable position, either on the floor or on a chair with your back straight. If you are sitting on a chair, try to ensure that your feet are flat on the ground. Have your hands resting in your lap or on the knees.

Begin by becoming aware of the breath as it enters in and then out through the nostrils.

Do not try to control the breath, only have the realisation that you are breathing.

Close your eyes, feel the breath as it flows gently in and out of your body.

As you take the next breath in through your nostrils allow it to become slower and deeper, as you breathe out, feel the muscles around your jaw, in your face and head relaxing. Breathe in slowly and deeply, filling the back, shoulders and neck, as you breathe slowly out relaxing and letting go of any tension. Take a long slow, deep inhalation all the way down to your tummy. As you exhale be aware of a feeling of relaxation. Take a deep breath in and notice a feeling of relaxation flowing into your arms, hands, legs and feet, as you exhale, the feeling of relaxation deepens.

Continue breathing slowly and deeply. Allowing each breath to take you deeper into a completely relaxed state of body and mind. If any feelings of stress or discomfort arise, notice where they are and how you are experiencing this present moment. Perhaps there is a heaviness, tightness, warmth or a tingling sensation somewhere in your body? Observe the thoughts and feelings without the need to follow nor analyse them.

In your minds-eye visualise or imagine that you are walking along a beautiful beach close to the ocean. Really get a sense of being there. Imagine the smell, sounds, feeling of soft sand beneath your feet as you walk slowly along the seashore. Feel the warm sunlight on your shoulders and a gentle breeze blowing through your hair. Visualise the waves and **imagine them lapping against the shore.** As the tide washes in, inhale. On the exhalation, follow the tide as it goes out and back into the depths of the sea.

Imagine that it is washing any feelings of tension, stress, anxiety and worry away from your body, dissolving them out into the vastness of the ocean.

When the mind starts to wander bring the attention back to the breath and the imagination watching the waves as they flow back and forth. Try to remain focused as the waves return to the shore, allow the breath to follow the waves taking an inhalation as they come in and exhalation as they return out into the sea.

Match the rhythm of your breath to the flow of the waves. If any distracting thoughts that come into your mind remain with the steady rhythm of your breathing and allow the unwanted thoughts to leave with the exhalation and the departing waves.

Take a long, slow deep breath in and exhale. Continue to remain with the breath as it flows in and out in-time with the waves. Each in-breath bringing you a feeling of peace and happiness, each out-breath releasing any remaining negativity. Continue in this way for a further 5 -10 minutes.

Take a deep breath in, hold for a moment, slowly exhale. Breathe in, hold, slowly exhale, take a deep breath in, hold and then slowly exhale. Bring your awareness back to the room and back to where you are seated. Wriggle your fingers and toes.

In your own time, without rushing, slowly open your eyes. Have a stretch. Resting for a few moments, and when you are ready, continue with the remainder of your day.

If practising this meditation at night you will be ready to go to sleep feeling wonderfully relaxed.

Meditation

Step Five: Releasing Negativity

Find a quiet place where you will not be disturbed, switch off your phone and focus your intention on wanting to relax. Ensure that the room is comfortably warm and give yourself this precious time to unwind. Sit in a comfortable position, either on the floor or on a chair with your back straight. If you are sitting on a chair, try to ensure that your feet are flat on the ground.

Begin by becoming aware of the breath as it enters in and then out through the nostrils. Do not try to control the breath, only have the realisation that you are breathing.

Close your eyes, feel the breath as it flows gently in and out of your body.

As you take the next breath in through your nostrils allow it to become slower and deeper, as you breathe out, feel the muscles around your jaw and in your face relaxing. Breathe in slowly and deeply, as you slowly breathe out feel your shoulders relaxing and letting go of any tension. Take a long, slow, deep breath in and as you slowly exhale feel your whole body letting go of tension anywhere in your body.

As the slow, deep breathing relaxes the body become aware of any thoughts. Take a deep inhalation and as you slowly exhale visualise that you are breathing out thick grey mist.

Imagine the smoke is your body's way of releasing any unwanted or negative thoughts. Follow the rhythm of the breath and continue breathing out worrying and stressful thoughts in the grey mist. Visualise or imagine the mist disappearing into space.

On your next in-breath visualise a white light above your head, as if the moon were directly above you and shining down onto you. Imagine that the white light gently flows in through the top of your head with the inhalation, filling your entire body from head to toes, this is a positive energy that is replacing the negative thoughts that you have released.

Take a long, slow deep breath in and visualise the white light filling your body, as you exhale allow any stressful thoughts or feelings to be released, imagine them being released contained in the grey smoke.

Take another long, slow, deep inhalation, visualise

the white light flowing into your body contained in the breath, as you slowly exhale release any remaining negative thoughts or feelings, imagine them being carried away in the grey mist that you exhale.

Continue breathing in white light and visualise it filling your body and releasing grey smoke on the exhalations for three more complete breaths. With each exhalation, the grey mist is fading away and getting lighter, until it has completely dissolved.

Relax your concentration, breathing naturally, wriggle the fingers and toes. When you feel ready and in your own time without the need to rush, slowly open your eyes. Relax for a few moments before returning to the rest of the day.

Meditation

Step Six: Golden Sunlight

Find a quiet place where you will not be disturbed, switch off your phone and focus your intention on wanting to relax. Ensure that the room is comfortably warm and give yourself this precious time to unwind. Sit in a comfortable position, either on the floor or on a chair with your back straight. If you are sitting on a chair, try to ensure that your feet are flat on the ground.

Begin by becoming aware of the breath as it enters in and then out through the nostrils. Do not try to control the breath, only have the realisation that you are breathing.

Close your eyes, feel the breath as it flows gently in and out of your body.

As you take the next breath in through your nostrils allow it to become slower and deeper, as you breathe out, feel the muscles around your jaw and in your face relaxing. Breathe in deeply, as you slowly breathe out feel your shoulders relaxing and letting go of any tension. Take a long, slow, deep breath in and as you slowly exhale feel your whole body letting go of any tension.

Allow the rhythm of the breath to settle, breathing in deeply and slowly, exhaling slowly. When you take the next slow, deep breath in, take a short pause before breathing out. Breathe in slowly and deeply, hold the breath for a moment, without straining, and then slowly exhale. Continue in this way with the three-point breathing, remembering to pause for a moment between the in and out breath. Proceed for several complete rounds, breath in, hold for a moment, and exhale.

Visualise or imagine that you are surrounded by a soft golden glow. Like a ray of sunlight that is above your head. As you breathe in slowly, try to imagine that this golden light is flowing in through the top of your head and filling your entire body. As your head fills with the sunlight it causes your face to light up with a soft smile. As the golden glow gently moves through your body it brings a feeling of warmth into your shoulders, arms and hands. As it continues to flow through your body the feeling of warmth moves down your back and into your tummy. Slowly the sensation fills the whole torso with a sense of warmth and peacefulness. Remember to continue breathing deeply in through your nostrils, pausing for a moment and then slowly exhaling.

The gentle glow moves down your legs into your feet and fills each of your toes with a feeling of warmth, it flows down your arms all the way to the fingertips.

Your whole body is feeling warm, deeply relaxed and pleasantly light. Imagine the warm gently glow is filling the heart centre in the middle of the chest. You feel calm, happy and you are becoming aware of the experience of inner peace.

Relax the rhythm of the breath and take a long, slow, deep breath in and slowly exhale. Wriggle the fingers and toes. Breathe naturally, and when you are ready, in your own time without the need to rush, slowly open your eyes.

Meditation
Step Seven: Breathing Body-Scan

We have learnt to become mindful about the breath using the three-point breathing exercise; it can help anchor us in the present moment and create a sense of peace and happiness. This version of the body scan will help deepen and develop a sense of mindfulness in the meditation practice.

Find a quiet place where you will not be disturbed. Switch off your phone, focus your intention and begin by telling yourself that you want to relax. Ensure that the room is comfortably warm and give yourself this precious time to unwind. Sit in a comfortable position, either on the floor or on a chair with your back straight. If you are sitting on a chair, try to ensure that your feet are flat on the ground.

Begin by becoming aware of the breath as it enters and then flows out through the nostrils. Do not try to control the breath, only have the realisation that you are breathing.

Close your eyes and feel the breath as it flows gently in and out of your body. Try to keep your attention at the area of your nostrils. As you continue to breathe mindfully allow the breath to become slower and deeper. As you breathe out feel the muscles around your jaw and in your face relaxing. Breathe in slowly and deeply, as you slowly exhale feel your shoulders relaxing and letting go of any tension. Take a long, slow, deep breath in and as you slowly exhale feel your whole body letting go.

Allow the rhythm of the breath to settle, breathing in deeply and slowly exhaling. As you breathe in, take a short pause before breathing out. Continue with the three-point breath in this way, remembering to pause for a moment between the in and out-breath. Bring the attention to the body and noticing how you feel in this present moment, even if it is a moment of fear, pain, sadness or even despair. Allowing the breath to move comfortably through the body without forcing or trying to control it. Silently give yourself permission to relax.

Focus your attention on the toes of both feet and be aware of how they feel. Try not to move them, only place your attention on any sensations. Do they feel warm, is there any coolness, tingling or perhaps you do not feel any sensations at all? Whatever you feel or do not feel is fine, remain mindful. With the next in-breath slightly tighten your toes, pause for a moment before you exhale and let go.

Bring your attention to both legs. Are you aware of any sensations? Just remain inquisitive as you scan your legs, from the ankles to the thighs. Breathe in slowly and tighten the muscles in your legs, hold the breath for a moment and on the slow exhalation release the tightness and feel the sensation as you breathe out and let go.

Move your attention into your tummy, pelvic area and lower back. Do you notice any tension in these areas? As you breathe slowly in, slightly tighten these parts of the body, hold and suspend the breath for a moment and be aware of how tightness feels. As you slowly exhale release and let go of any tightness in the muscles.

Breathing slowly and deeply into your shoulders, chest, upper back and neck, slightly tighten these areas. Be aware and notice this feeling. Suspend your breath for a moment, and as you slowly exhale notice the difference in the sensation as you let go of the tightness and relax with the out breath.

Scan down your arms, hands and into the fingers. Breathe in deeply and slowly. Make your hands into tight fists and imagine holding onto tension, suspend your breath with the fist for a moment. As you slowly breathe out allow your hands to open and release the tightness that you were holding on to. Remain mindful.

Bring your awareness into your face and head. Notice the tiny muscles around the eyes, and mouth, how do they feel? Be curious about the muscles in your jaw and temples. How do they feel? Be aware of any sensations in your face. Take a long, slow, deep breathe in and tighten the muscles in your face, hold the tension with the suspended breath for a moment. Tighten the muscles in the face a little bit more, and then slowly let go as you breathe out. Feel the difference between holding tension and relaxing. Notice how you feel. Allow the face and head to completely relax.

Take a long, slow, deep breath in through the nostrils and allow it to flow all the way down to your toes. Hold for a moment and then as you slowly exhale feel, imagine or visualise the breath coming up from your toes and moving through the entire body and slowly out through the nostrils. Repeat, this process breathing slowly, and deeply in through the nostrils, imagine, visualise that the breath is flowing down to your toes, hold for a moment and slowly exhale returning the breath up through the body and out through the nostrils.

Repeat for the third time. Breathing slowly and deeply, following the breath with your awareness all the way down to the toes. Suspend the breath here for a moment and slowly exhale imagining the breath is moving up through your body and out through the nostrils.

Relax your concentration, wriggle your fingers and toes. When you are ready, in your own time without rushing slowly open your eyes. Relax for a few moments before continuing with the rest of your day.

Meditation

Step Eight: The Tree

Find a quiet place where you will not be disturbed, switch off your phone and focus your intention on wanting to relax. Ensure that the room is comfortably warm and give yourself this precious time to unwind. Sit in a comfortable position, either on the floor or on a chair with your back straight. If you are sitting on a chair, try to ensure that your feet are flat on the ground. Place your hands in your lap or on the knees.

Close your eyes and allow your attention to focus on the breath, breathing naturally and not trying to control it in any way. Allow the body to relax, feel the shoulders letting go of any tension. Feel the face relax, feel the arms and hands relaxing. As you continue to breathe naturally allow the tummy, back, legs and feet to relax. If the mind begins to wander, try not to follow the thoughts and return your attention to the breath.

Stay focused on the breath, as it slowly enters in through the nostrils, allowing the breath to fill the heart area in the centre of the chest. Hold the breath at the heart for a moment and as you slowly exhale release any worrying thoughts from your mind. Take a long, slow, deep breath in, suspending at the heart for a moment and then as you slowly exhale release any tension from anywhere in the body. Take another long, slow, deep breath in, hold at the centre of the chest and as you slowly exhale let go of any anxiety. Allow the rhythm of the breath to settle in this pattern and take another long, slow, deep breath in to fill the heart centre, hold for a moment and keep your concentration focused without straining. Slowly exhale and let go of any negative states of mind such as anger, jealousy, resentment or irritation, that may be troubling you.

You are drifting deeply into a more relaxed state of mind and any thoughts are floating away like clouds. Do not follow them only observe and each time that a cloud appears bring the attention back to the breath.

Now that you are feeling totally relaxed visualise if you will, in your mind's eye, or just imagine that it is a beautiful sunny day, and you are walking in the forest. Notice the trees towering above and lining the path ahead of you, they are covered with an abundance of leaves that are fresh and green. Hear the sweet sound of birds singing from high in the treetops.

The path weaves its way before you. The sunlight glistens as it streams between the tangled web of branches. You notice one tree and you feel drawn towards it. This is the tallest and most beautiful tree that you have ever seen. You sense the welcoming energy, a vibration that is emanating from the trunk, branches and leaves. As you move closer imagine yourself merging with the tree.

The tree has a strong life-force, imagine that you reach your arms up high and they seem to merge into the branches stretching up towards the sky. In your mind's eye see your fingers blending into the leaves and your legs and feet into the roots. With your mind and imagination follow the roots as they go down deep into the earth. This sensation causes you to feel grounded and strong. The energy of the tree moves up from its roots and through the trunk, continue to be one with the tree. The energy moves into the branches and the leaves. A feeling of strength moves through your body. You feel the warmth of the sunlight that is directly above your head and it gently moves down from the top of the tree in through the crown of your head, into the branches and flowing into your arms and hands, down the trunk through your back and legs into your toes and the roots of the tree. You feel strong as the warm sensation and the energy of the tree moves through your body; continuing to flow down to the roots keeping you grounded and secure.

Take a deep breath in, focus your attention as the breath flows down to your toes. Hold the breath with the feeling of warmth for a moment, and as you slowly exhale the breath moves up through the body and out through the nostrils. Be aware of the feeling of warmth leaving the nostrils. Continue breathing slowly and deeply following the breath as it moves down through the tree and down to the roots, hold for a moment and then slowly exhale and enjoy the warm feeling as it flows through the tree and through your body and out from your nostrils. You feel so relaxed.

Take a deep breath in, hold the breath for a moment, as you slowly exhale move away from the tree and imagine that you are walking back along the path that brought you to this place. You can return here anytime that you need to feel strong and grounded.

Relax the concentration and breathe naturally. Wriggle your fingers and toes and bring your awareness back to the place where you are seated.

In your own time, without needing to rush and when you feel ready, slowly open your eyes; rest for a while before returning to the activities of the day.

Meditation
Step Nine: The Mountain

Find a quiet place where you will not be disturbed, switch off your phone and focus your intention on wanting to relax. Ensure that the room is comfortably warm and give yourself this precious time to unwind. Sit in a comfortable position, either on the floor or on a chair with your back straight. If you are sitting on a chair, try to ensure that your feet are flat on the ground. Place your hands in your lap or on the knees.

Close your eyes and allow your attention to focus on the breath, breathing naturally and not trying to control it in any way. Allow the body to relax, feel the shoulders letting go of any tension. Feel the face relax, feel the arms and hands relaxing. As you continue to breathe naturally allow the tummy, back, legs and feet to relax. If the mind begins to wander, try not to follow the thoughts and return your attention to the breath. Be aware of the breath as it enters in and then out through the nostrils.

Close your eyes and focus on the breath as it flows gently flows through your body.

As you take the next breath in through your nostrils allow it to become slower and deeper, hold the breath for a moment and as you breathe out feel the muscles around your jaw and in your face relaxing. Breathe in slowly and deeply, hold the breath for a moment, as you slowly breathe out feel your shoulders relaxing and letting go of any tension. Take a long, slow, deep breath in, hold for a moment or two and as you slowly exhale feel your whole body letting go of any tension.

Allow the breath to settle in this rhythm, breathing in deeply and slowly, holding for a count of three and then slowly exhaling. Continue in this way for three more full breaths, remembering to pause for a count of three between the in and out-breath.

Recall and visualise a tall mountain, maybe it is a place that you have visited, seen in a picture, or it is one that you can create in your imagination. You imagine yourself standing at the base of the mountain. Many paths are leading up the sides. Pause for a moment and allow your intuition to guide you towards the path that you would like to take. The object is to reach the summit and how you experience the climb is up to you. If you feel any tension anywhere in your body breathe into it using the three-point breath. Breath in, hold for a moment and slowly exhale releasing any stress, anxiety, worries, pain or fears from the body and mind. Feel your shoulders letting go and relaxing.

Continue to scan your body searching for areas of tension and tightness, any parts that feel uncomfortable breathe deeply into those areas, hold for a count of three and then slowly release, letting go of the tension with the out breath and imagining it dissolving away into space. Breathe into each area of the body until all the tension has been dissolved.

Now that you are feeling calm and relaxed you are ready to choose the path that will take you to the top of the mountain.

The path that you have chosen is filled with trees and streams, at first it appears to be very steep and difficult to climb. But you continue to ascend, determined to reach the top. Be aware of everything around as you continue to climb higher and higher. Are there any obstacles on the path ahead, or does it look clear and welcoming?

As you continue to climb you hear the faint sound of birds singing as if they were cheering you on to reach the summit. Be mindful and notice if is it daytime, or have you been climbing for so long that it is now almost nightfall? How does the sky look, what are the colours, are there any clouds or is it a clear sky?

You have left all the stress, worry, pain, fears and anxiety at the base of the mountain and as you climb higher you begin to feel lighter and lighter. Your breath feels calm and deep and each breath is helping you to climb the path. As you continue to climb you hear a babbling brook as it tumbles down the side of the mountain, rolling over rocks and stones. With an intense curiosity you wonder where had the watery torrent started. There are thick clumps of long grass swathed in the muddy ground.

You look up and see that you have almost reached the top. How does it look? Is it pointed, is the peak covered with snow, are there any trees, or is it almost a flat surface? Will you be able to sit and rest when you have reached the summit?

Perhaps you are struggling to reach the summit, but there are only a few more steps to climb. Keep going and use the breath to help your ascent. As you reach the top of the huge mountain a feeling of exhilaration fills your body and mind. And you take your first step onto the summit. You look down the side of the mountain and notice how steep and rugged the path was. But you have done it and you feel empowered.

There is a large boulder, you sit down and rest. Look at the wondrous scenery that surrounds you. Through your effort and determination, you can witness this view. It looks almost like a landscape painting with vibrant colours and shapes. You take a long slow breath all the way in through your nostrils and feel the breath as it flows throughout your body. It creates a feeling of deep inner peace and as the breath fills your heart centre suspend your breathing for a count of three, you feel happy and blissful as you slowly exhale and the feeling of happiness seems to be all around. There is a vibration that resonates at your heart centre. A cool breeze gently swirls around, and you sense that you are completely connected to all of nature.

Breathe in deeply and hold at the heart centre with the feeling of calmness, slowly exhale. Breathe in deeply and hold at the heart centre with a feeling of creativity, slowly exhale. Breathe in deeply, hold at the heart centre and with a feeling of courage. You know that the struggle to reach the top was worth the effort.

Be mindful of the surroundings, your thoughts and feelings. Take a long slow deep breath in, and slowly exhale. Breathe effortlessly in and slowly exhale. Continue to breathe naturally for a few moments.

On the next out-breath start to wriggle your fingers and toes. Bring your awareness back to the room and where you are seated. In your own time without rushing, open your eyes and have a stretch. Release a long sigh. Relax for a few moments. Spend a little time to jot down anything that you remember from the meditation. When you feel ready continue with your daily routine.

Sunset over Primrose Hill, May 2020.

Meditation
Step Ten: Floating in Space

Find a place where you will not be disturbed and switch off your phone. Ensure that the room is comfortably warm and give yourself this precious time to unwind. If would be helpful to have a sheet of paper and pen at hand, this will allow you to write down, after the meditation, any experiences that occurred. If you have a specific question that needs clarification or guidance, jot it down on the paper now and you can bring it to mind during the meditation. Focus your intention on wanting to relax.

Sit in a comfortable position, either on the floor or on a chair with your back straight. If you are sitting on a chair, try to ensure that your feet are flat on the ground. Place your hands in your lap or on the knees.

Close your eyes and allow your attention to focus on the breath, breathing naturally do not try to control it in any way. Allow the body to relax, feel the shoulders letting go of any tension. Feel the face relax, feel the arms and hands relaxing. As you continue to breathe naturally allow the tummy, back, legs and feet to relax. If the mind begins to wander, try not to follow the thoughts and return your attention back to the breath. Be aware of the breath as it enters in and then out through the nostrils. Focus on the breath as it flows gently flows through your body.

As you take the next breath in through your nostrils allow it to become slower and deeper, hold the breath for a moment and as you breathe out feel the muscles around your jaw and in your face relaxing. Breathe in slowly and deeply, hold the breath for a moment, as you slowly exhale feel your shoulders relaxing and letting go of any tension. Take a long, slow, deep breath in, hold for a moment or two and as you slowly exhale feel your whole body letting go of any tension. Allow the breath to settle in this rhythm, breathing in deeply and slowly, holding for a count of three and then slowly exhaling. Continue in this way for three more full breaths, remembering to pause for a count of three between the in and out- breath.

In your mind's eye imagine or visualise that you are walking along the beach, it is a warm summer's evening, the tide is out, and the sand stretches for miles until it joins the sea. The sun is beginning to set over the distant horizon, notice the colours of the sky, crimson, pink and royal blue.

Further along the beach, you see a cliff and you head towards that direction.

When you reach the foot of the cliff you find a path and you follow it up effortlessly. Higher and higher you climb; with each step you are feeling lighter and lighter. Breathing gently and naturally. Continue climbing until you reach the top. The sun has now set, and the sky is turning to a shade of rich indigo blue. You look up at the vastness and are in awe at the wonders of the universe. Bright stars twinkle like diamonds that are scattered across the night-time sky.

A cool breeze swirls around, you look down and on a nearby rock there is a blanket, pick it up and wrap it around your shoulders. It feels safe and warm. Notice the colour of the blanket. Take a long, slow deep inhalation, hold for a count of three, exhale. Take a long, slow deep breath in, hold for a count of three, exhale, you are feeling lighter and more relaxed than you have ever felt. Take another long, slow, deep breath in, hold for a count of three, slowly exhale.

You notice that your feet are feeling light, your legs are feeling lighter, the torso is feeling lighter, arms and hands so much lighter, your face and, neck and head are feeling lighter, the whole body has a sensation of lightness and you feel your mind expanding as if you are floating out into space, you feel safe and deeply relaxed. Please, be aware that you can return to the cliff anytime that you choose but for now, continue to feel relaxed as you float, almost like a cloud.

Continue breathing gently and naturally. Imagine yourself floating in the darkness surrounded by the stars. It is beautiful and you have an awareness that you can expand your mind farther out into space. Until you see a star that feels in alignment and you have a connection. The star holds the ancient wisdom of the universe. If there is a question that you may have been searching for an answer, think about it now and focus on this issue. Allowing yourself to trust and believe that the universe will provide you with an answer. Visualise the bright, white sparking light from the star that is directly above you. The white light surrounds you and flows through you, creating a sense of peacefulness, relaxation and happiness.

Slowly and gently breathe into this feeling, hold for a count of three and then slowly exhale. Take another slow, deep breath in, hold for a count of three and then slowly exhale. One more slow, deep inhalation, hold for a count of three, slowly exhale. Focus your concentration on the question that you are asking.

The universe has heard, and knows the answer to your question, you will receive that wisdom. Be aware that you may not get the answer immediately, however, it will arise in your mind. Be open to receiving.

Visualise the white light and bring it into the centre of your chest. Breathing gently and naturally. You begin to gradually return, floating back towards the cliff. You feel deeply relaxed, safe, calm and peaceful. Your awareness slowly and gradually returning to your body and then into the room.

Take a deep breath in, and slowly exhale, breathe in and slowly exhale, take a deep breathe in, hold and then slowly exhale. Relax your concentration. Wriggle your fingers and toes. Breathing gently and naturally. In your own time without the need to rush, slowly open your eyes. Remain seated for a few moments and allow your mind the time to process the experience.

At this point you may wish to jot some down some key points that come to mind from the meditation. For example, do you remember the blanket that you wrapped yourself in when you were on the clifftop? What was the colour? Do you remember the question that you were asking and focused on? Did you write it down before the meditation? Do you have any insights or answers arising in your mind?

How do you feel following the meditation? Are you feeling lighter, more relaxed, happier?

It is essential to keep notes and compare them with the next time that you practice this meditation. Please be aware that an answer to your question may not be obvious straight away. However, it may appear in your mind at any time during the next day or even the next few weeks, be sure that it will arise.

The more that we develop our awareness the more open we will become to receiving guidance. All the answers to all our questions are within each one of us and we only need to learn how to ask and listen.

Afterword

Have you ever thought about meditation and said, it will not work for me? Well, you are not alone.

That is why this practical and easy to learn ten-step course has been developed to guide us along the path. It all starts with the breath because we all breathe, but do we realise how powerful the breath is?

This readable book and recorded meditations will help us to begin by taking the first steps on a meditation journey. Information about the download recordings available to accompany this course can be found in the contact details at the end of the book.

Glossary

Firewalking Has been practised by many people from different cultures for thousands of years. The action of walking barefoot over hot coals requires the participant to go into deep meditation, it is an inspirational journey that creates a feeling of empowerment and self-achievement.

Creative Visualisation The process of using imagery to generate a mental image and stimulate perception. It is used by people from many walks of life and for a variety of reasons. In meditation, it is used to enhance the imagination and increase relaxation. Sportspeople utilize it to improve their performance and it can be used to transform negative beliefs into positive attitudes and behaviour.

TM An abbreviation for *Transcendental Meditation*. It is a form of meditation whereby a person relaxes and clears the mind by the silent repetition of a special word that is called a mantra and it is given to the practitioner by their teacher.

Mindfulness This encourages one to focus on an awareness of the feelings and sensations that are being experienced in the present moment.

Three-Step Breath A certain way of breathing, consisting of three specific breaths to improve concentration and help the person to deeply relax.

TSM The abbreviation for *Ten Step Meditation*. This course has been developed for the beginner in meditation and provides a complete program starting with the basics of the breathing meditation and is completed with an advanced level that uses visualisation to create a sense of inner peace and happiness.

MBSR Abbreviation for *Mindfulness-Based Stress Reduction* is an eight-part program that uses a type of meditation and teaches a person to focus on the present moment by being fully aware of what is happening both within and externally.

Talking Therapy The focus is on helping a person manage their problems by changing the way that they think.

Mantra A meaningful word or sentence that is repeated over and over to help the body and mind become calm.

Breath-work A type of breathing where you intentionally change the pattern of the breath to help improve well-being and clarity of the mind.

Focus single-pointedly Concentration on a single object, without movement, to train the mind.

About the Author

Linda T Levine is an inspiring and experienced meditation guide. She has been practising for more than three decades and has worked with internationally renowned experts and masters from the UK and USA.

She has twenty years of practical experience as a natural health consultant and educator. She is passionate about helping people to learn and understand the benefits of meditation.

Over the years, her interest in how the mind works have led to extensive investigation and personal experiences into the power of thought.

Contact details

The complete course, including all ten guided meditation recordings, are available to download. For more information about the Ten Step Meditation Path, please contact:

Email: info@makemeditationmatter.co.uk

Additional guided meditations are available to download and include:
Secret Moon, Lavender Meditation, Crystal Journey, The Tree.

Website: www.makemeditationmatter.co.uk

The Willow Tree

My roots grow strong and deep

The Hamptons, Long Island

The rhythm of the breath flows like the waves

Medical Disclaimer

Whilst meditation is a safe method in helping to alleviate stress and negative states of mind, it is essential that it is not used to replace medication nor medical advice. If you are currently receiving medical care, please consult with your healthcare practitioner before commencing this or any form of mindfulness meditations.

Printed in Great Britain
by Amazon

55133091R00048